W9-BZX-310

DISAPPEARING ACTS

Three-toed Sloths
Green Mammals

by Natalie Lunis

Consultant: Adriano G. Chiarello, Ph.D.
Graduate Program in Vertebrate Zoology,
Catholic University of Minas Gerais, Belo Horizonte, Brazil;
Member of the Anteaters, Sloths and Armadillos Specialist Group of the IUCN

BEARPORT
PUBLISHING

NEW YORK, NEW YORK

Credits

Cover, © Shane Partridge/Fotolia, and © Les Cunliffe/ Fotolia; TOC, © worldswildlifewonders/Shutterstock; 4, © Michael Fogden/Oxford Scientific/ Photolibrary; 5, © Gerry Lemmo/www.gerrylemmo.com; 6L © Michael & Patricia Fogden/Minden Pictures; 6R, © Gerry Ellis/Minden Pictures; 7TL, © Michael & Patricia Fogden/Minden Pictures; 7BL, © Bill Hatcher Photography; 7TR, © Thierry Montford/Foto Natura/Minden Pictures; 7BR, © age fotostock/SuperStock; 8, © Nick Gordon/Photolibrary; 9, © Joel Sartore/NGS Image Collection; 10, © Norbert Wu/Minden Pictures; 11, © Gaertner/ Alamy; 12L, © Brian Kenney/Getty Images; 12TR, © Prisma/SuperStock; 12BR, © Wildlife/Peter Arnold Inc.; 13, © Norbert Wu/Science Faction; 14, © Michael & Patricia Fogden/Minden Pictures; 15, © worldswildlifewonders/Shutterstock; 16, © Michael & Patricia Fogden/Minden Pictures; 17, © Wayne Lynch/Photolibrary; 18T, © Anup Shah/NPL/Minden Pictures; 18B, © age fotostock/SuperStock; 19, © age fotostock/SuperStock; 21, © Michael & Patricia Fogden/Minden Pictures; 22L, © Mark Moffett/Minden Pictures; 22C, © Steve Hopkin/Ardea; 22R, © Premaphotos/Nature Picture Library; 23TL, © Gaertner/Alamy; 23TR, © worldswildlifewonders/Shutterstock; 23CL, © Christoph Achenbach/iStockphoto; 23CR, © iStockphoto; 23BL, © Gerry Lemmo/www.gerrylemmo.com; 23BR, © Adam Siegel.

Publisher: Kenn Goin
Editorial Director: Adam Siegel
Creative Director: Spencer Brinker
Design: Kim Jones
Photo Researcher: Picture Perfect Professionals, LLC

Library of Congress Cataloging-in-Publication Data

Lunis, Natalie.
  Three-toed sloths : green mammals / by Natalie Lunis.
      p. cm. — (Disappearing acts)
  Includes bibliographical references and index.
  ISBN-13: 978-1-936087-42-6 (library binding)
  ISBN-10: 1-936087-42-1 (library binding)
  1. Bradypus—Juvenile literature. I. Title.
  QL737.E22L86 2010
  599.3'13—dc22

                              2009032629

For more information, write to Bearport Publishing Company, Inc., 101 Fifth Avenue, Suite 6R, New York, New York 10003. Printed in the United States of America in North Mankato, Minnesota.

112009
090309CGC

10 9 8 7 6 5 4 3 2 1

Contents

Covered in Green

In a thick, green forest, many tall trees grow.

Long, tangled vines cling to them.

Tiny plants grow on the **bark** of their trunks and branches.

Don't be fooled, however.

Some of the greenish bark isn't what it seems to be.

It's a slow-moving animal called a three-toed sloth!

A three-toed sloth's greenish fur acts as **camouflage**, making the animal hard to see.

Hanging Around

Three-toed sloths spend almost all their time in trees.

Sometimes they hang upside down from tree branches.

They use their large, hook-like **claws** to hold on tight.

claws

There are four kinds of three-toed sloths. All of them live in thick, green forests in Central and South America.

Where Three-toed Sloths Live

Brown-throated sloth

Pygmy sloth
(lives on an island in Central America)

Pale-throated sloth

Maned sloth

NORTH AMERICA

Atlantic Ocean

Central America

Pacific Ocean

SOUTH AMERICA

Panama

Slow Eaters

A sloth sleeps most of the day.

When it wakes up, it starts pulling itself from branch to branch, looking for leaves, twigs, and buds to eat.

It doesn't have to hurry, and it doesn't need to go far.

Many sloths stay in the same small area of trees all their lives.

The three-toed sloth is one of the world's slowest **mammals**. It usually takes a sloth one minute to travel seven feet (2 m). That's the same distance a person walks in three steps.

Animal or Plant?

Many tiny plant-like living things called **algae** are able to grow on a sloth's **coat**.

Together, the tiny algae form big greenish patches on the sloth's brown fur.

Because of these patches, the sloth blends in well with the green and brown branches it hangs from.

Algae grow well in the wet, rainy forests where sloths live.

algae

algae

Safe in the Trees

Blending in with branches helps protect the sloth.

Meat-eaters such as jaguars, big harpy eagles, and snakes called anacondas would attack and eat one if they saw it.

They rarely do, however—especially because the hidden sloth moves around so little and so slowly.

jaguar

anaconda

harpy eagle

If a sloth is found by an enemy, it uses its huge, sharp claws to try to defend itself.

13

Down on the Ground

Sloths stay safe in the trees, but they are always in danger when they are on the ground.

Their weak back legs are not built for running or walking.

The only way a sloth can get around on the ground is by using its front claws and strong front legs.

Little by little, it drags itself along on its belly.

Surprisingly, though, sloths are good swimmers.

a sloth swimming

Sloths come down to the ground for only one reason— to pass waste from food and water out of their bodies. Luckily, they need to do so only about once a week.

15

Mother and Baby

Sloths can sleep and eat while hanging upside down.

Female sloths even give birth that way.

A mother sloth has one baby at a time.

As soon as it is born, the baby crawls onto its mother's belly and hangs on to the hair of her brown and green coat.

baby sloth

mother

A baby sloth already has large, hook-like claws when it is born. It uses the claws to crawl over its mother's fur.

17

Growing Up Slowly

For the first two months of its life, a baby sloth drinks milk from its mother's body.

Then it starts to eat food from the trees as well.

It keeps hanging on to its mother, riding slowly among the treetops.

By watching her, the baby learns which leaves, twigs, and buds are good to eat.

Sloths live in trees like monkeys, but they are not related to monkeys. Instead, they are related to anteaters and armadillos.

anteater

armadillo

Brown, Green, and Grown-Up

A baby sloth stays with its mother until it is about nine months old.

After that age it no longer needs to live with her.

The young sloth's brown fur has turned greenish.

It can now drop out of sight and start safely hanging around on its own.

Scientists aren't sure exactly how long three-toed sloths live. They think the animals live for about 12 years— possibly longer.

More Disappearing Acts

Three-toed sloths aren't the only creatures that hide by looking just like the trees they live in. Here are three more animals that are camouflaged to look like parts of trees.

Praying Mantis

Leaf Insect

Gecko

Glossary

algae (AL-jee) tiny plant-like living things that grow in water or on damp surfaces

claws (KLAWZ) sharp nails at the ends of the fingers or toes of an animal

bark (BARK) the tough covering on a tree

coat (KOHT) an animal's fur

camouflage (KAM-uh-flahzh) colors and markings on an animal's body that help it blend in with its surroundings

mammals (MAM-uhlz) warm-blooded animals that have a backbone, hair or fur on their skin, and drink their mothers' milk as babies

Index

Read More

Guidone, Julie. *Sloths.* Pleasantville, NY: Weekly Reader (2009).

Lang, Aubrey. *Baby Sloth.* Markham, Ontario: Fitzhenry & Whiteside (2004).

Miller, Sara Swan. *Sloths (Paws and Claws).* New York: Rosen (2008).

Learn More Online

To learn more about three-toed sloths, visit
www.bearportpublishing.com/DisappearingActs

About the Author

Natalie Lunis has written many science and nature books for children. She hides out among the leaves and trees in the Hudson River Valley, just north of New York City.